# STREET FOOD OF INDIA

Published in 2010 by I.B.Tauris & Co Ltd
6 Salem Road, London W2 4BU
175 Fifth Avenue, New York NY 10010
www.ibtauris.com

Distributed in the United States and Canada Exclusively by
Palgrave Macmillan
175 Fifth Avenue, New York NY 10010

First published in India by Roli Books, 2009

ISBN: 978 1 84885 420 8

A full CIP record for this book is available from the British Library
A full CIP record is available from the Library of Congress

Library of Congress Catalog Card Number: available

Printed and bound in Singapore

# STREET FOOD
# OF INDIA

## THE 50 GREATEST INDIAN SNACKS –
## COMPLETE WITH RECIPES

Sephi Bergerson

I.B. TAURIS

LONDON · NEW YORK

# contents

# introduction

Early morning in a sweet-shop. Eye-catching 'Jaipur pink' boxes of *ghevar* (a crisp sweet made of flour) are freshly prepared and packed as two women wait for customers in a sweet store in a buzzing Jaipur by-lane.

**Preceding page 1:** An array of biscuits on display, with teacups perched on the jars, in a restaurant window, Kolkata.

**Preceding pages 2-3:** A vendor selling pineapples on a rickety wooden cart in Old Delhi.

**Preceding page 5:** Balancing act: A hawker carries a tray of *Ram ladoos* (fried mixed gram fritters) on his head and a portable stand on his shoulder in Lodi Gardens, New Delhi.

In the main bazaar of Pahar Ganj, a popular area amongst backpackers who visit Delhi, there is a *pakora* (fritters) stand that's been there since the beginning of time. A fat man used to run it, at the corner of the vegetable market, selling *pakoras* for ten rupees a plate. He sat—and is probably still sitting—cross-legged on a high platform over the black oil, and all he did through the day was to prepare the highly favoured snack. You could choose the combination you wanted—*aloo, gobi, baingan, palak* or *piaz* (potato, cauliflower, eggplant, spinach or onion)—and he would serve it on a leaf plate topped with green chutney that could burn your mouth if it was the first time you'd tried it.

This is the first food I ever ate in India after I descended from a so-called 'hotel' to explore what I thought was India. I had arrived that morning on an early flight from Tel Aviv and was welcomed to the rousing main bazaar by the *neem datun* (toothbrush) vendors and wandering cows. I had no idea what Indian *chai* (tea) tasted like but I had to try the *pakora*. After the first tongue-burn and runny nose, I was hooked.

A few years later, I was married and living in Israel. After more than ten years as an advertising and commercial photographer it became clear to me that something had to change. The advertising world is a lot about planning, strategy, markets, budgets, commercial approach and sometimes a lot of fun; but it cannot work without a constant stream of new ideas and exposure to the outside world. What I needed was a new approach to my work. I had always wanted to be a documentary photographer and India was beckoning me ever since that first *pakora* in Pahar Ganj. I was lucky that my wife was happy to follow me but it was not until we had had our baby daughter that we actually made the move

Golden and green lemons ready to be squeezed to make refreshing *nimbu pani* (lemonade). Water-carts, such as this one, are a boon during the harsh Indian summers.

to India. We both felt at home in Delhi from the time we landed at the Indira Gandhi international airport and this feeling hasn't changed since—even after almost seven years in this amazing country. The face of Delhi, my new abode, is rapidly changing but it continues to feel like home to us.

Back to the *pakora-wala*. A little more than a year after we came to Delhi, I got a call from someone in Tel Aviv for an 'India story' for a food magazine. I had to suggest an idea and street food was the first thing I could think of. He got excited and asked me to start shooting.

Somehow, the story never happened but I liked the images I had shot till then and decided to keep going. The whole exercise became an exploration of colour and texture. I was looking at the various dishes almost as abstract colours and figures within the subject, with the fascination of someone looking for jewels and gemstones hidden in rubbles of dust. Orange *jalebis*, crispy *aloo tikkis* and white-green-maroon *dahi bhallas* were suddenly transformed into heroes of a magical world that lay hidden just before my eyes, waiting to be found.

Time and the opportunity to travel to other cities revealed new worlds and new variety in street food. Having *kachori* on the ghats near the river Ganga in Varanasi was nothing like having it in Old Delhi, or anywhere else for that matter. Mumbai's *vada pao* was not the *aloo chop* of Raipur. Even bread *pakora* had so many variations.

In time, I became almost obsessed as the language of the streets and this amazing phenomenon started opening up to me. The places where I ate grew more and more important as I started developing a taste for certain dishes. Whenever in Mumbai, for example, I could not go a day without the simple sweet 'three-rupee *nimbu pani*', that simplest of lemonades at the railway station, and would almost religiously go to Nariman Point for a 'veg sandwich'. Oh, how tasty simple bread with vegetables can be!

As I went deeper into the subject, I began to feel that a book would be the ultimate product of this photographic process. While magazines, newspapers and galleries are indeed fantastic places to exhibit one's work, once a book is born it has a life of its own and shows the photographer's wider view and definition of the subject. More than a single print or a magazine story, a book lives on in perpetuity and reaches a larger audience with a bigger and more complete body of work that has evolved and matured.

My decision to work on such a long-term project allowed me to move around the subject and watch my style develop and change with time. And so, from close-up shots of orange *jalebis* diamonds and sweet *paans* I zoomed out and started looking at the stalls and the people that came to eat there. Textures of food items started making way for facial expressions as I was trying to capture the delight of eating on the street.

People in India are very friendly and every traveller would testify to that. They love to make conversation with foreigners and most of the time they love having their picture taken (especially when you want them out of the frame). I am not an Indian and, at least in the way I look, I will always be a foreigner in India. This can prove to be a disadvantage at times, especially when dealing with rickshaw- or taxi-drivers or trying to buy things. I am asked to pay double, or more, of what a local would pay for the same service or item, but I found that a little bit of Hindi and a smile always helps make things a bit more accessible.

What is obvious in the eyes of an Indian who knows the culture can easily elude a foreign photographer who is not aware of its intricacies and does not know what to expect and where to put the emphasis. On the other hand, this can become an advantage as certain things that are so much a part of daily life escape the attention of the local and yet can be eye-catching and amazing for an outsider. Street food is a fantastic example of being an omnipresent feature of urban India that has largely escaped the attention of photographers here.

I've been shooting street food for more than four years now and, living in Delhi, I have learned the alleyways of Chandni Chowk, Old Delhi's legendary market area, and its wonders by heart. From makeshift kitchens on the roadside or a mobile eatery assembled on a cart or bicycle, to snack-sellers carrying their wares in baskets around the busy lanes—on nearly every street in the city someone is selling some tasty and inexpensive food. Over time I have started recognizing people and the names of my favourite places and have started taking my friends and visitors to feast at Parathe Wali Gali and to Natrang Dahi Bhalla Wala.

Changing seasons in India bring different dishes out on the stands. *Jamoon* fruit in summer, sweet potato in winter, *gajar ka halwa* on a cold night in Old Delhi and sweet *lassi* on a hot summer morning in Jaipur. And *chai*, of course . . . the *chai* is everywhere. At four in the morning, waiting for the train, I had it in a small glass; in Kolkata in an earthen pot that was then smashed to the ground; and in Gujarat from a small plate. This is the blood that flows in the veins of the streets in India. Boiled, mixed and poured—with ginger or without, cardamom or not, normal sweet or way too sweet—thick with milk and spices. Like a god of the streets, people know it by many names but revere it equally. *Chah* in Punjab, *cha* in the north east, *chaha* in the hills, *chai* across north India, 'cutting' in Bombay, *chaya* in pockets of Rajasthan, it is all but a cup of tea, but if you've ever had it you'd know that there is tea and there is *chai*.

It was on one of these many visits to Old Delhi, one winter night that I found it. Just below the massive stairs on the eastern side of the great Jama Masjid lies Meena Bazaar, a local market of cosmetics, pictures and posters of sacred places, readymade *burqas*, embroidered caps and other items, mostly for use by the Muslim community in the area. A few metres away from the small food stalls and *dhabas* selling mostly non-vegetarian delicacies, stands what is arguably the greatest of all *chai* stalls in India.

Now don't get me wrong; I admit I have had better *chai* in many other places in India, but at Ustad Chai Stall it is all about the show used to create what I started calling the *chai-wala's* unique 'chai latte'.

Three huge teapots are always boiling over the blazing furnace and the *chai-wala* assistant is constantly mixing sweetened, thickened, creamy hot milk in a huge *kadhai* to make a rich and thick foam. Around fifty glasses are placed on the counter at one go and the crowd of young boys, waiting to take *chai* to their bosses in the nearby shops, are almost jumping over one another's heads in anticipation of being first to secure the prized liquid. Sugar comes first, thrown into the glasses with tremendous speed, '*chak . . . chak . . . chak*', and then the hot teapot takes a low flight over the glasses, filling them with black tea without spilling a single drop. Mixing the sugar and tea is a noisy process and only then comes the milk. One by one, each glass is topped with the frothy cream of hot milk and, whoever's hand reaches closer—holding a small empty cup—gets the first *chai* glass right into the empty cup. If you have no empty cup in your hand it is obvious you are not a regular. The old-timers come prepared so as not to be forced to hold the hot glass in their hands. The *chai* itself is a mild one, very low on spices and equally light in taste. But the gimmick of the glasses inside the cup, the brown tea, the whitish foam, the crowded alley, the sweat and excitement of the crowd—the sheer spectacle of the preparation—makes for one of India's most unforgettable *chai* experiences.

Having grown up in Israel, a country that, like India, has gone through many changes in recent decades, I understand that nothing is permanent. I have seen the horse-carts and the vendors of the prickly Sabra fruit disappear from the streets of my hometown and it has always been clear to me that the street food of India will go the way of the Ambassador car. That old model that has been in production since 1957 was once considered India's national car and used to be the preferred means of conveyance for India's political leadership, before they moved on to SUVs and luxury cars. The same way, people who earlier had their lunch at the local *dhaba*, now flock to the new international fast food chains that have sprouted everywhere.

For the people of India, street food is an everyday thing, something they could no more imagine the cities being without than the sacred cows on the streets of Delhi. Nevertheless, as incomes rise and ways of eating change, the inevitable is happening and the street-side treats may soon be a thing of the past. Street food, that symbol of wild, chaotic, urban India, is slowly being harnessed. In recent years, it has begun to come indoors, get sterilized, go upmarket. A famous restaurant in the posh south Delhi colony of Vasant Vihar now serves *golgappa* with vodka. One newspaper defined it as the 'South Delhification of Purani Dilli's chatpata chaat', referring to the centre of social gravity moving south from Old Delhi to the newer parts of the city. This is expectedly bringing about a major change in some of Old Delhi's famous street recipes that are being driven away from their place of origin.

To the amazement of inhabitants of Delhi, in early 2007, as part of a plan to clean up the Indian capital's streets, the Supreme Court passed an order to ban cooking at stalls along the roadside. The authorities were

Mouth-watering *bread pakoras* (a batter-fried snack stuffed with a mixture of vegetables and cottage cheese) stacked up invitingly in a shop on the streets of Amritsar.

A *moongphalli* (groundnut) vendor awaits customers on Chowpatty Beach, Mumbai.

concerned that street food was cooked and served in filthy, unsafe conditions, and wanted it cooked under standardized conditions within four walls and sold pre-packed.

The nature of street-side setups is that there is little room for storage and vendors make enough food only for one day. It may be prepared at home or on the street over a gas or charcoal fire, but circumstances dictate that the food is always fresh. It can prove to be difficult to the preconceptions of Westerners, and indeed to many 'educated', city-bred Indians, who insist on 'sanitized' meals, but such concerns are belied by the immense popularity of street food in India. People who buy from street vendors may do so out of economic necessity, but they can be as discerning about their choice of food as those who can afford to dine in restaurants.

Street food forms a small-scale industry that provides employment to hundreds of thousands of people in Delhi, many of whom are illiterate. From the masterful brewers of masala *chai* on street corners to the new immigrants stirring up spicy curries from their home villages, it is estimated that the equivalent of millions of US dollars change hands every day through the sale of street food in the major cities of India.

Street food has always been popular but is becoming even more important in urban India as it provides inexpensive and nutritious meals to customers from a variety of economic backgrounds, and to workers who face increasingly long commutes. If this recent decision by the Supreme Court is enforced, more than 300,000 hawkers could be forced to close their outdoor kitchens. The disappearance of the *chhole bhature* guy and his bicycle from these busy streets would be one of the most unfortunate fallouts of the seismic shift that is taking place in Delhi's modern fabric.

But if you visit India now, it is still here. Food on the trains in India is already changing, but thankfully the night trains going through the biggest state—Uttar Pradesh—that stop in smaller towns will still be the centre of mercantile attention for the *puri aloo* vendors and the *chai-wala's*. If you are in a regular sleeper class train from Varanasi to Delhi you will surely be woken up to their calling, '*puri puri puriiiiiii . . . chai chai chayeeeee . . .*' for a while longer yet.

The cup that cheers: 'Come oh come ye tea-thirsty restless ones – the kettle boils, bubbles and sings, musically'.

Rabindranath Tagore.

*Chah* in Punjab, *cha* in the Northeast, *chaha* in the hills, *chai* across the north, *cutting* in Mumbai, *chaya* in pockets of Rajasthan, all denote a cup of tea, the hot beverage omnipresent across India, bringing streets and railway platforms alive.

**Left:** Gurmeet Singh presides over Giani Tea Stall on Circular Road, Amritsar. Note the unique handle of the utensil used to brew the ambrosia of hot, sweet tea.

**Far Left:** A *chaiwala* (tea vendor) near the railway station in Raipur.

**Right:** Fresh, thick *lassi* (yoghurt drink) poured into *kulhars* (clay cups) on M.I. Road, Jaipur.

**Far Right:** Two young men stack up crushed ice and *kulhars* next to a popular *lassi* shop on M.I. Road, Jaipur.

# MEETHI LASSI  sweet yoghurt drink  serves: 5-6

## Ingredients

| | |
|---|---|
| Yoghurt (*dahi*), | 2 cups / 500 gm / 1.1 lb |
| Sugar | 2 tbsp / 30 gm / 1 oz |
| Water, cold | 4 cups / 1 lt / 32 fl oz |
| Cream | 1 tbsp / 15 ml |
| Ice cubes, crushed | |

## Method

1. Blend the yoghurt, sugar and water until frothy. Top with thickened cream and crushed ice. Serve at once.
2. For some variation, mix any fruit with the above.

A street vendor and his young, playful assistant near Mohammed Ali Road, Mumbai. Rs 2 is all you need for a glass of *masala chaach* (buttermilk), and Rs 3 if you fancy a glass of *meethi lassi*.

# VADA PAO indian potato burger

## Ingredients

| | |
|---|---|
| Potatoes, boiled, peeled, mashed | 4 |
| Gram flour (*besan*) | 2 cups / 200 gm / 7 oz |
| Salt to taste | |
| Turmeric (*haldi*) powder | 1 tsp / 3 gm |
| Garlic (*lasan*) cloves | 2 |
| Ginger (*adrak*) | 1" |
| Green coriander (*hara dhaniya*), chopped | 1 cup / 50 gm / 1¾ oz |
| Onions, chopped | 2 |
| Vegetable oil for deep-frying | |
| Bread (*pao*) | |

## Method

1. Mix the gram flour with salt and turmeric powder. Add enough water to make a batter of medium-thick consistency.
2. Grind the garlic and ginger to paste and add to the mashed potato along with green coriander and onions. Mix well.
3. Divide the mixture equally into small dumplings.
4. Heat the oil in a wok (*kadhai*); deep-fry the dumplings till golden brown.
5. Now coat the dumplings with the batter and fry again till golden brown. Remove and drain the excess oil on absorbent kitchen towels.
6. Split the *pao* into half keeping the base intact. Place the dumplings inside and serve.

Luscious green coconuts filled with refreshing coconut water at a stall, Mumbai.

A stall selling *vada pao* (the poor man's burger, one of the most popular street snacks of Mumbai), and other snacks outside the busy Dadar railway station, Mumbai. *Vada* is a potato dumpling deep-fried in oil, and *pao*, which came to Maharashtra from neighbouring Goa, is very similar to Portuguese bread (Goa used to be a Portuguese colony).

A vendor piling freshly-baked loaves of bread on his arm as another man sneaks into the camera frame for his moment of fame, Kolkata.

A hawker selling cotton sugar uses a hand bell to announce his arrival, Kolkata.

Plump *mirchi vada* on the streets of Jaipur. Stuffed chillies are dipped into batter and deep-fried to make a fiery snack.

# MIRCHI VADA deep-fried stuffed green chillies

## Ingredients

| | |
|---|---|
| Green chillies, long, fat, slit lengthwise | 4 |

**For the stuffing:**

| | |
|---|---|
| Potatoes, medium-sized, boiled, mashed | 2 |
| Cumin (*jeera*) seeds | ½ tsp / 1 gm |
| Dried pomegranate seeds (*anar dana*) | 1 tsp / 3 gm |
| Dried mango powder (*amchur*) | 1 tsp / 3 gm |
| Salt to taste | |
| Green coriander (*hara dhaniya*), chopped | a handful |
| Ginger (*adrak*), grated | 1" |

**For the batter:**

| | |
|---|---|
| Gram flour (*besan*) | 1 cup / 100 gm / 3½ oz |
| Salt | ½ tsp |
| Baking powder | ¼ tsp |

Vegetable oil for deep-frying

## Method

1. **For the stuffing**, mix all the ingredients together and divide the mixture into 4 portions. Stuff each portion into the green chillies.
2. **For the batter**, mix all the ingredients together adding enough water to make a batter of medium-thick consistency.
3. Heat the oil in a wok (*kadhai*); coat each chilli with the batter and fry on medium heat until golden brown and crisp. Repeat till all are fried.
4. Serve hot with green relish (see p. 79).

**Left:** A man selling *idli* (a south Indian steamed cake made of fermented rice) near Dadar railway station, Mumbai. The fresh banana leaves will be used as plates.

**Far Left:** Benaras, or Varanasi, is renowned for its *jalebis* (sweet flour whirls) and *kachoris,* (savoury deep-fried pastries) available round the clock in the famous Kachori ki Gali (Kachori Lane). Or you can head for the *ghats* (river bank) where appetizing *kachori* and *aloo subzi* (potato curry) can be teamed up with a view of the Ganges river for as little as Rs 5.

# IDLI  steamed rice cakes

serves: 4

## Ingredients

| | |
|---|---|
| Rice, parboiled | 3 cups / 600 gm / 22 oz |
| Split black gram (*urad dal*) | 1½ cups / 300 gm / 11 oz |
| Fenugreek seeds (*methi dana*) | 1 tsp / 4½ gm |
| Salt to taste | |

## Method

1. Soak the rice in water for 40 minutes and the split black gram for 20 minutes (the water level should be way above the rice).
2. Grind separately the rice and the split black gram (add the fenugreek seeds when grinding the split black gram). Both should be finely ground.
3. Mix the two batters with salt and keep aside to ferment for 10-12 hours. Keep in a warm place for it to rise.
4. Pour the batter into the receptacles in the *idli* plates and steam in a cooker for 7 minutes. Repeat till all the batter is used up.
5. Serve hot with coconut chutney (see below).

# NARIYAL CHUTNEY  coconut chutney

serves: 4

## Ingredients

| | |
|---|---|
| Coconut (*nariyal*), grated | 1 cup / 100 gm / 3½ oz |
| Salt to taste | |
| Green chillies, chopped | 2 |
| Water, cold | ½ cup / 125 ml / 4 fl oz |
| Vegetable oil | 1 tsp / 2 ml |
| Black mustard seeds (*rai*) | ½ tsp / 1½ gm |
| Fenugreek seeds (*methi dana*) | ½ tsp / 2¼ gm |

## Method

1. Blend the coconut, salt and green chillies with water for a minute.
2. Heat the oil in a pan; add the black mustard and fenugreek seeds. When they start crackling, pour this tempering over the coconut mixture. Mix well.
3. Serve cold.

**Note:** You can also blend everything together in a blender for 2 minutes and keep in a cool place.

# ALOO KACHORI stuffed potato patties

## Ingredients

| | |
|---|---|
| Refined flour (*maida*) | 3½ cups / 500 gm / 1.1 lb |
| Salt | 1 tsp / 4 gm |
| Ghee | 4 tbsp / 60 ml / 2 oz |
| Yoghurt (*dahi*) | 2 tbsp / 30 ml / 1 oz |
| Water, chilled | ½ cup / 125 ml / 4½ fl oz |
| Green chillies, deseeded, finely chopped | 2-3 |
| Ginger (*adrak*), finely chopped | ½ tbsp / 7½ gm |
| Potatoes, boiled, mashed | 300 gm / 11 oz |
| Coriander (*dhaniya*) powder | 1 tsp / 3 gm |
| Cumin (*jeera*) powder | 1 tsp / 3 gm |
| Fennel (*saunf*), ground | ½ tsp |
| *Garam* masala | 1 tsp / 3 gm |
| Turmeric (*haldi*) powder | a pinch |
| Lemon (*nimbu*) juice | 1 tbsp / 15 ml |
| Salt | 1 tsp / 4 gm |
| Green coriander (*hara dhaniya*), finely chopped | 2 tbsp / 8 gm |
| Vegetable oil for frying | |

## Method

1. Mix the flour and salt in a mixing bowl. Add ghee, rub until fully incorporated and the mixture resembles coarse breadcrumbs. Add yoghurt and 6 tbsp chilled water; knead to make a smooth and pliable dough. Cover with plastic wrap and keep aside for half an hour.
2. Combine the remaining ingredients except oil in a mixing bowl and knead with hands until well blended. Divide into 18 portions; keep aside.
3. Divide the dough equally into 18 portions. Shape each portion into a patty. Cover with a damp towel or plastic wrap and set aside.
4. Flatten each patty into a 2½" or 6 cm round. Place one portion of the filling in the centre of the dough, then bring the sides of the dough over the filling to enclose completely. Pinch the seams together until thoroughly sealed. Cover with a plastic wrap or a moist towel. Keep aside. Shape and stuff the remaining patties.
5. Heat the oil in a wok (*kadhai*) till it starts smoking. Slide in a few patties (seam-side down) at a time. Fry until pale golden in colour and until they sound hollow when tapped. The crust should be delicately blistered and crisp. Remove and drain excess oil and serve hot, accompanied by tomato ketchup.

Two men push a sugarcane juice cart (*ganna*, or *ankh* in Bengali) on the streets of Kolkata. The recycled yellow vegetable oil container is filled with water for washing dirty glasses.

Fresh sugarcane at a juice stall in Kolkata.

A freshly painted poster, portraying two Bollywood stars, Ajay Devgan (left) and Karishma Kapoor (right), brightens a juice stall in New Delhi.

Juice stalls in Delhi are a painter's delight. The classic style of painting is still alluring, surviving stiff competition by quicker and more cost-effective methods of sign painting now available in India.

**Right:** An invitation to slake thirst: A stall near the UPSC (Union Public Service Commission) building in New Delhi.

**Far Right:** Red grapefruit peeled and cleaned for sale as a snack in Rishikesh.

# PHALON KA RAS    mixed fruit juice

serves: 4-6

## Ingredients

| | |
|---|---|
| Sweet lime juice (*mausami*) | 2 cups / 500 ml / 16 fl oz |
| Pomegranate (*anar*) juice | 2 cups / 500 ml / 16 fl oz |
| Pineapple (*ananas*) | 2 slices |
| Sugar to taste | |
| Water | 1 cup / 250 ml / 8 fl oz |
| *Chaat* masala to taste | |

## Method

1. Blend all the ingredients together with crushed ice.
2. Sprinkle *chaat* masala and serve immediately.

---

# AAM LASSI  mango yoghurt drink

serves: 2-3

## Ingredients

| | |
|---|---|
| Mango (*aam*), peeled, chopped | 2 |
| Yoghurt (*dahi*) | 2 cups / 500 gm / 1.1 lb |
| Cold milk | ½ cup / 120 ml / 4 fl oz |
| Sugar | 2 tsp |
| Vanilla essence, optional | ¼ tsp |

## Method

1. Blend all the ingredients together with crushed ice until smooth.
2. Serve chilled.

**Note:** You can substitute the mango with papaya or very ripe bananas to make papaya *lassi* or banana *lassi* respectively.

An antiquated scale used to weigh *dahi* (yoghurt) at a stall in Delhi. The towering metal object in the background is a mixer-blender to make *lassi*, a yoghurt drink.

Flavoured *lassi* in different colours is served for breakfast near Dadar railway station, Mumbai.

# DAHI BHALLA black gram dumplings in tangy yoghurt serves: 6

## Ingredients

**For the *bhalla* (dumplings):**

| | |
|---|---|
| Split black gram (*urad dal*) | 1 cup / 200 gm / 7 oz |
| Water | 2 cups / 500 ml / 16 fl oz |
| Salt | ½ tsp |
| Cumin (*jeera*) seeds | 1 tsp / 2 gm |
| Ginger (*adrak*), chopped | 2 tsp |
| Green chillies, chopped | 1 tsp |
| Vegetable oil | 1¼ cups / 300 ml / 10 fl oz |

**For the yoghurt mixture:**

| | |
|---|---|
| Yoghurt (*dahi*), thick, whisked | 2 cups / 500 gm / 1.1 lb |
| Sugar | 1 tsp |
| Salt | ½ tsp |
| Cumin seeds, roasted, pounded | 1 tsp / 2 gm |
| Black salt (*kala namak*) | ½ tsp |
| White pepper (*safed mirch*) powder | ½ tsp |

**For the garnishing:**

| | |
|---|---|
| Ginger, julienned | 1 tsp |
| Green chillies, julienned | 1 tsp |
| Green coriander (*hara dhaniya*), chopped | 1 tbsp / 4 gm |
| Red chilli powder | a pinch |
| Cumin seeds, roasted, pounded | a pinch |
| Mint (*pudina*) leaves | 4 sprigs |
| Tamarind chutney (*sonth*, see p. 167) | |

## Method

1. **For the *bhalla*,** clean the black gram and soak in water for 2 hours. Drain and grind to fine paste, adding very little water. Remove to a mixing bowl and add salt, cumin seeds, ginger, and green chillies. Mix well and shape into even-sized balls.

2. Heat the oil in a wok (*kadhai*); add the prepared balls, a few at a time, and deep-fry till golden brown. (Make a hole in the centre of the ball with the thumb just before frying.) Remove and drain the excess oil on absorbent kitchen towels.

3. Soak the prepared *bhalla* in lukewarm water till soft.

4. **For the yoghurt mixture**, add all the ingredients and mix well.

5. Remove the *bhalla* from water, squeeze out excess water and add to the yoghurt mixture. Keep aside for 10-15 minutes.

6. Serve chilled, garnished with ginger, green chillies, green coriander, red chilli powder, cumin powder, mint leaves, and tamarind chutney.

*Dahi bhalla* is an elaborate snack popular across India. An assortment of flavours, with a tangy mix of spices to give the taste buds a roller coaster ride! A permanent fixture at all *melas* (fairs), it is also found frequently on the street side.

A street vendor in Pushkar, Rajasthan, cooking *malpua*. Dipped into a syrup of water, sugar and sweet lime, *malpua* is a sweet delicacy made of condensed milk, semolina, plain flour and *gur* (jaggery).

*Aloo chaap* is a potato snack in central India. A famous stand near the railway station in Raipur does brisk business.

# ALOO CHOP stuffed potato dumplings

## Ingredients

| | |
|---|---|
| Potatoes | 350 gm / 12 oz |
| Beetroot (*chukander*) | 100 gm / 3½ oz |
| Green peas (*hara mater*), shelled | 100 gm / 3½ oz |
| Sweet potatoes (*shakarkandi*) | 100 gm / 3½ oz |
| Cauliflower (*phool gobi*) | 50 gm / 1¾ oz |
| Vegetable oil | 5 tbsp / 50 ml / 1¾ fl oz |
| Onion, chopped | 2 tbsp / 24 gm |
| Ginger (*adrak*) paste | 1 tbsp / 18 gm |
| Garlic (*lasan*) paste | 1 tbsp / 18 gm |
| Turmeric (*haldi*) powder | 1 tsp / 2 gm |
| Red chilli powder to taste, optional | |
| Raisins (*kishmish*) | 50 gm / 1¾ oz |
| Green chillies, sliced | 1 tbsp |
| Salt to taste | |
| *Garam* masala | 1 tbsp / 9 gm |
| Eggs, beaten | 2 |
| Breadcrumbs | 1 cup / 120 gm / 4 oz |
| Vegetable oil for deep-frying | |

## Method

1. Boil and mash all the vegetables together. Keep aside.
2. Heat the oil in a wok (*kadhai*); add the onion and sauté till brown. Add the ginger-garlic pastes and cook till the oil comes to the surface. Add the turmeric powder and red chilli powder, if desired, and then the mashed vegetables. Keep stirring for a few minutes.
3. Mix in the raisins, green chillies, salt and *garam* masala. Remove and keep aside to cool.
4. When cool enough to handle, divide the mixture equally into lemon-sized balls. Shape each portion either into balls or egg shapes. Dip them in egg, roll in breadcrumbs and keep aside.
5. Heat the oil in a wok; carefully lower the balls and deep-fry until uniformly brown. Remove with a slotted spoon and drain the excess oil on absorbent kitchen towels.
6. Serve with tomato chutney or tomato sauce.

**Note:** For pure vegetarians, if you do not wish to use egg, then make a batter with 3 tbsp cornflour and some water, and then dip the balls in this batter instead of egg.

Quenching thirst with water next to a food stall in Varanasi. Drinking water is an art in India as people manage to drink without touching their lips to the glass.

# MALPUA   fried sweet pancakes

## Ingredients

| | |
|---|---|
| Wholewheat flour (*atta*), sieved | 1 cup / 150 gm / 5 oz |
| Sugar / Jaggery (*gur*) | 3 tbsp / 45 gm / 1½ oz |
| Aniseed (*saunf*), coarsely ground | 1 tbsp / 7½ gm |
| Black peppercorns (*sabut kali mirch*), coarsely ground | 1 tbsp / 12 gm |
| Yoghurt (*dahi*) | 2 tbsp / 30 gm / 1 oz |
| Milk | 1 cup / 240 ml / 8 fl oz |
| Ghee | 2 cups / 500 gm / 1.1 lb |
| Water as required | |

## Method

1. To the flour, add sugar, aniseed, and black pepper. Mix well. If using jaggery, rub till the flour and yoghurt are well mixed.
2. Add milk and enough water to make a batter of pouring consistency.
3. Heat the ghee in a flat-bottomed non-stick pan till smoking hot. Take a ladleful of the batter and pour into the pan. The batter should spread itself. If it doesn't, then add a little more water and mix well.
4. Cook till the pancake sides turn golden brown. Remove with a perforated ladle and drain on absorbent kitchen towels. Serve hot.

---

# SUJI HALWA   semolina pudding

## Ingredients

| | |
|---|---|
| Semolina (*suji*), coarse | 2 cups / 200 gm / 7 oz |
| Salt | ½ tsp |
| Sugar | ½ cup / 110 gm / 3½ oz |
| Water | 1 cup / 250 ml / 8 fl oz |
| Ghee / Vegetable oil | 4 tbsp / 60 gm / 2 oz |
| Groundnuts (*moongphalli*) | 30 gm / 1 oz |

## Method

1. Prepare the sugar syrup by boiling the water and sugar together. Keep aside.
2. Heat the ghee or oil in a wok (*kadhai*); add the groundnuts and fry for 30 seconds. Add the semolina, mixed with salt and stir-fry until light brown. Pour in the sugar syrup and cook until it is absorbed, taking care that the mixture does not become too dry.
3. Serve hot.

# RAM LADOO fried mixed gram fitters

## Ingredients

| | |
|---|---|
| Bengal gram (*chana dal*) | 2 cups / 400 gm / 14 oz |
| Split black gram (*urad dal*) | ½ cup / 100 gm / 3½ oz |
| Salt to taste | |
| Black pepper (*kali mirch*) to taste | |
| Ginger (*adrak*), grated | 1 tbsp / 18 gm |
| Green chillies, finely chopped | 2-3 |
| Asafoetida (*hing*) | a pinch |
| Green coriander (*hara dhaniya*), finely chopped | a bunch |
| Vegetable oil for deep-frying | |

## Method

1. Wash and soak the grams separately for 4-5 hours. Drain and grind separately to a coarse and grainy paste.
2. Now mix both the gram pastes along with the remaining ingredients (except oil) together.
3. Heat the oil in a wok (*kadhai*); gently lower spoonful of mixture into the oil and fry the balls till crisp and golden brown. Remove and drain the excess oil on absorbent kitchen towels. Repeat till all the mixture is used up.
4. Serve hot with green chutney (see p.79).

---

# PAKORA vegetable fritters

## Ingredients

| | |
|---|---|
| Potato, large, peeled, sliced | 1 |
| Aubergine (*baingan*), small, sliced | 1 |
| Onion, large, sliced | 1 |
| **For the batter:** | |
| Gram flour (*besan*) | 2 cups / 200 gm / 7 oz |
| Salt | 1 tsp / 4 gm |
| Red chilli powder | 1 tsp / 3 gm |
| Baking powder | ½ tsp |
| | |
| Vegetable oil for frying | |

## Method

1. In a bowl, combine all the ingredients for the batter. Mix well, adding a little water to make a very thick batter.
2. Heat the oil in a wok (*kadhai*); dip the sliced vegetables into the batter, one at a time, and deep-fry until crisp and golden brown. Remove with a slotted spoon and drain the excess oil on absorbent kitchen towels.
3. Serve hot with tomato sauce.

*Farari chevada* – a potato dish decorated with red pomegranate seeds in Ahmedabad.

**Right:** A street scene in Varanasi. The town is a snack paradise, although hygiene is suspect, the eateries being little more than gaps in a wall; or benches and *charpais* (string cots) spread around a cauldron of frying pans, filled with smouldering oil.

**Following pages 54-55:**
**Left:** *Chai* time: *Chai* is probably the most popular beverage across India.
**Right:** An old man holding a *kulhar* (clay cup) of hot *chai* near Sadar Street in Kolkata. Clay cups are the 'paper cups' of India, an estimated 17 million (1.7 crore) *kulhars* being consumed in India every day. The Railway Ministry is trying to double the production of *kulhars* to over 30 million (3 crore) a day by making them more user-friendly so that people thirsty for tea at railway stations and in trains are not disappointed.

A man preparing chowmein (fusion Indian-Chinese noodles) at a food stall selling Chinese food in Kolkata.

People fill up water containers on the street next to a food stall selling *chhole bhature* (spicy chickpeas served with fried leavened bread), Kolkata.

# BHATURE  deep-fried leavened bread

## Ingredients

| | |
|---|---|
| Refined flour (*maida*) | 2 cups / 280 gm / 10 oz |
| Soda bicarbonate | ½ tsp |
| Salt | a pinch |
| Sugar | 1 tsp / 4 gm |
| Yoghurt (*dahi*) | 4 tbsp / 60 gm / 2 oz |
| Water, warm | 5-6 tbsp / 75-90 ml / 2½-3 fl oz |
| Ghee, melted | 1 tsp / 4 gm |
| Vegetable oil for deep-frying | |

## Method

1. Mix the refined flour with soda bicarbonate and salt. Sieve into a bowl. Add sugar, yoghurt and enough warm water and knead into a smooth dough. Knead till the dough stops sticking to the fingers or to the sides of the bowl. Grease your palms with 1 tsp ghee and continue to knead till the dough becomes pliable. Cover with a moist cloth and keep aside in a warm place or over a pan of warm water for 3½-4 hours.
2. Divide the dough into 10 equal parts; shape into balls and roll out discs of 10 cm or 4" in diameter. Keep them covered on a tray.
3. Heat the oil in a wok (*kadhai*) to smoking point; deep-fry the discs, one at a time, till it puffs up and turns light golden. Remove with a slotted spoon and drain the excess oil on absorbent kitchen towels.
4. Serve hot with *chhole* (see p. 59).

# CHHOLE  spicy chick peas

## Ingredients

| | |
|---|---|
| Chick peas (*kabuli chana*), soaked overnight | 2 cups / 300 gm / 11 oz |
| Tea bag or tea dust wrapped in muslin cloth | 1 or 1 tsp |
| Vegetable oil | ½ cup / 120 ml / 4 fl oz |
| Gram flour (*besan*), sifted | 1 tbsp / 10 gm |
| Coriander (*dhaniya*) powder | 1 tbsp / 9 gm |
| Red chilli powder to taste | |
| Turmeric (*haldi*) powder | 1 tsp / 3 gm |
| Ginger (*adrak*), julienned | 1 tbsp / 7½ gm |
| *Garam* masala | 1 tsp / 3 gm |
| Salt to taste | |
| Mango powder (*amchur*) | 1 tsp / 3 gm |

**For the garnishing:**

| | |
|---|---|
| Onion, sliced | 1 |
| Green chillies, slit lengthwise | 4 |
| Potatoes, boiled, peeled, diced | 2 |
| Lemon (*nimbu*), cut into wedges | 1 |

## Method

1. Pressure cook the drained chick peas with 2 cups water and tea bag or tea dust wrapped in muslin cloth for 10 minutes or until soft. Drain and reserve the water.
2. Heat the oil in a wok (*kadhai*); fry the gram flour, coriander and red chilli powders for 2 minutes. Add the chick peas, reserved water, turmeric powder, ginger, *garam* masala and salt. Cook for 4-5 minutes. Add the mango powder and simmer for another 3 minutes.
3. Remove and garnish with onion, green chillies, potatoes and lemon wedges. Serve hot with *bhature* (see p. 58).

**Left:** A man eats *idlis* (south Indian snack made of fermented rice) for lunch near Writers Building in Kolkata, next to a make-shift temple of the goddess Durga. According to a survey conducted in the city, it is estimated that in Kolkata alone there are about 130,000 street food vendors offering highly nutritious food at unbelievably cheap rates.

**Far Left:** *Dahi bhalla* (black gram dumplings in tangy yoghurt sauce), a north Indian snack, decorated with chilli peppers and tomato slices on the streets of Hyderabad.

**Following pages 62-63:**
**Left:** A painted signboard advertising a milk drink in Mumbai.

**Right:** Movie posters lean against the wall in a small alley and a *bhisti* (water-carrier) serves water out of a mussock or goatskin, slung over his shoulder, Kolkata.

A hawker pouring syrup over crushed ice on a stick to make a *gola* (ice-cream concoction), Bhuj.

**Left:** A young girl buying a *gola* on a hot summer day near Bhuj. *Gola* or *chuski* is the poor man's ice-cream, it is basically crushed ice with flavoured syrup.

*Ganna* (sugarcane) juice vendor, Assam.

Sugarcane placed on a banana leaf and sold on the road in West Bengal, about 40 kilometres south of Kolkata. In these remote villages, it is a favourite sweet snack of children.

An ice vendor distributing ice to the vegetable shops in the narrow lanes of Old Delhi.

**Left:** Lavishly garnished cold *lassi* chilled in glasses on ice in Moradabad. The ready-to-serve glasses stand in a hole in a metal box containing ice.

A man serves *dosa* (stuffed savoury pancake made of fermented rice and pulses) at a south Indian food stall in Khao Gali (food lane), Mumbai. *A dosa* is the Indian equivalent of the French crépe – although it is only served as a savoury dish.

# MASALA DOSA stuffed savoury pancakes

## Ingredients

**For the batter:**

| | |
|---|---|
| Rice, parboiled or any other ordinary rice, soaked overnight | ¾ cup / 150 gm / 5 oz |
| Black gram (*urad dal*), soaked overnight | ¾ cup / 150 gm / 5 oz |
| Fenugreek seeds (*methi dana*) | ¾ tsp |
| Salt to taste | |

**For the filling:**

| | |
|---|---|
| Potatoes, boiled, peeled, roughly mashed with fingers | 400 gm / 14 oz |
| Vegetable oil | 2 tbsp / 30 ml / 1 fl oz |
| Black mustard seeds (*rai*) | 1 tsp / 3 gm |
| Fenugreek seeds | ½ tsp / 1½ gm |
| Onion, finely sliced | ¾ cup / 180 gm / 6 oz |
| Turmeric (*haldi*) powder | 2 tsp / 6 gm |
| Red chilli powder or | ½ tsp / 1½ gm |
| Green chillies, finely chopped | 2 |
| Ghee / Vegetable oil for frying | |

## Method

1. **For the batter,** drain and blend the rice to a semi-thick paste. The paste should feel a bit grainy.
2. Drain and blend the black gram with the fenugreek seeds to a fine paste. Mix the two pastes together and let the mixture stand overnight. Mix salt to taste.
3. **For the filling,** heat the oil in a wok (*kadhai*); add the mustard and fenugreek seeds. When they start crackling, add the onions. Sauté for a while, then add the turmeric powder, mashed potato and red chilli powder or green chillies. Fry for a minute. Keep aside.
4. Heat a non-stick frying pan; pour a ladleful or rounded spoonful of the batter in the centre. Spread the batter in a circular motion with the back of the spoon to cover the surface. Allow it to cook on medium heat until the underside is golden, spreading some ghee or oil in the centre and along the sides.
5. Place 2 tbsp of the potato filling in the centre, spread it along the radius and gently fold the pancake from the 2 sides. Sprinkle a little more ghee or oil. Serve at once with coconut chutney (see p. 30).

**Note:** You can refrigerate the leftover batter in an airtight container for future use. This will keep fresh for up to 3 weeks.

# PHAL KI CHAAT mixed fruit delight

## Ingredients

| | |
|---|---|
| Apples (*seb*), cored, diced | 2 |
| Pears (*nashpati*), cored, diced | 2 |
| Banana (*kela*), peeled, thickly cut | 1 |
| Papaya (*papita*), peeled, deseeded, diced | ½ |
| Mango (*aam*), peeled, diced | 1 |
| Potato, large, boiled, peeled, diced | 1 |
| Cucumber (*khira*), peeled, diced | 1 |
| Lemon (*nimbu*) juice | 1 tsp / 5 ml |
| Black salt (*kala namak*) | 2 tsp |
| Red chilli powder | ½-1 tsp / 1½-3 gm |
| Mint (*pudina*) paste | 1 tsp / 5 gm |
| Tamarind (*imli*) pulp | 1 tsp / 5 gm |
| *Chaat* masala | 1 tsp / 5 gm |

## Method

1. Mix all the fruits and vegetables together in a bowl.
2. Add lemon juice, black salt, and red chilli powder. Mix and keep aside for 10 minutes.
3. Serve with a dressing of mint paste mixed with tamarind pulp and *chaat* masala.

**Note:** 1 tsp lightly roasted and powdered cumin seeds may also be added. This preparation must be made fresh almost before being served to retain the crispness of the fruits. Any combination of seasonal fruits may be used.

**Right:** A vegetable vendor near Lahori Gate in Old Delhi. Fresh vegetables seasoned with *chaat* masala and black salt are eaten separately or as a mixed plate as vegetable or fruit *chaat*.

**Far Right:** A vendor makes a long cut in a radish, just before sprinkling spicy *chaat* masala on it. Fresh vegetables sold on the streets as snacks are always sprayed with a mix of fruit masala, salt and fresh lemon juice.

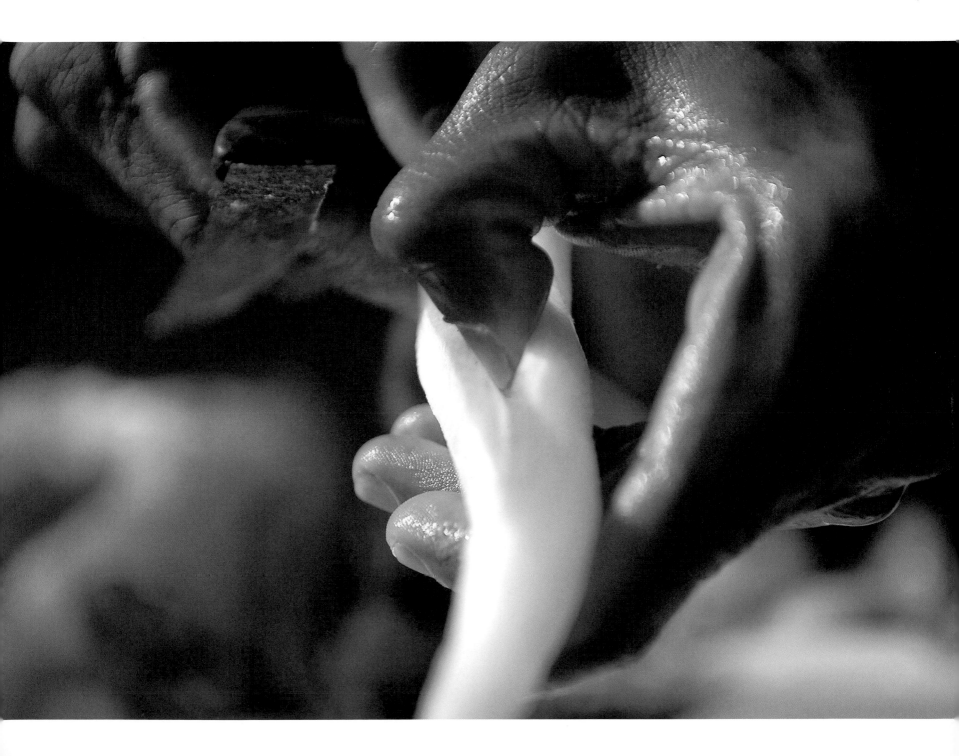

**Right:** The famous Mumbai grilled vegetable sandwich.

**Far Right:** Students from a nearby college enjoy the Mumbai vegetable sandwich at Khao Gali (food lane), Mumbai.

# MUMBAI VEGETABLE SANDWICH

makes: 2

## Ingredients

| | |
|---|---:|
| Brown bread | 4 slices |
| Cucumber (*khira*) | 1 |
| Tomato | 1 |
| Beetroot (*chukandar*) | 1 |
| Butter to taste | |
| Green chutney (see p. 79) | 1 tbsp / 15 gm |
| Salt | a pinch |
| Black pepper (*kali mirch*), grounded | a pinch |
| Ketchup to taste | |

## Method

1. Peel the beetroot and cook in water until soft but crisp. Thinly slice the cucumber, tomato and beetroot.
2. Butter both sides of the bread slices. Spread one side with a generous amount of green chutney and then pile a few slices of cucumber, beetroot and lastly tomato.
3. Sprinkle with salt and pepper and cover with another slice of bread and put into the toaster until golden.
4. Remove and top with some more green chutney and ketchup.

# HARA DHANIYA CHUTNEY coriander relish

serves: 4-6

## Ingredients

| | |
|---|---|
| Green coriander (*hara dhaniya*), washed thoroughly with roots removed, chopped | 3 cups / 150 gm / 5 oz |
| Onions, peeled, chopped | 50 gm / 1¾ oz |
| Garlic (*lasan*) clove, peeled, chopped | 1 |
| Green chilli, chopped | 1 |
| Water | ½ cup / 125 ml / 4 fl oz |
| Salt to taste | |
| Sugar | 2 tsp / 6 gm |
| Lemon (*nimbu*) juice | 2 tsp / 10 ml |

## Method

1. Grind or blend the green coriander with onions, garlic, green chilli and water.
2. Add the salt, sugar and lemon juice. Mix well.
3. Serve at room temperature or cold with kebabs.

---

# PUDINA CHUTNEY mint relish

serves: 4-6

## Ingredients

| | |
|---|---|
| Mint (*pudina*) leaves, washed | 4¼ cups / 150 gm / 5 oz |
| Onions, peeled, chopped | 60 gm / 2 oz |
| Green chillies, chopped | 2 |
| Sugar | 2 tsp / 6 gm |
| Lemon (*nimbu*) juice | 2 tsp / 10 ml |
| Salt to taste | |
| Water | ½ cup / 125 ml / 4 fl oz |

## Method

1. Grind or blend together the mint leaves with the remaining ingredients.
2. Serve cold or at room temperature.

**Left:** A man extracting juice on the road in New Delhi.

**Far Left:** An array of tempting fruit in splendid colours decorating a juice stall, Kolkata.

**Right:** A decorated water-cart, a common sight on the streets of New Delhi, offering chilled water for just 50 paisa.

**Far Right:** Pale yellow fresh limes decorate a water-cart selling refreshing *nimbu pani* (lemonade).

**Left:** A hawker sells bananas stacked in baskets on his bicycle under a shop sign in a posh market in central Delhi.

**Far Left:** A street scene in New Delhi. A sweet potato vendor talks to a friend sitting on the ground next to his portable stall.

# SAMOSA  triangular vegetable patties

## Ingredients

**For the pastry:**

| | |
|---|---|
| Refined flour (*maida*) | 3½ cups / 500 gm / 1.1 lb |
| Salt to taste | |
| Vegetable oil | ¼ cup / 60 ml / 2 fl oz |
| Water to knead | |

**For the filling:**

| | |
|---|---|
| Ghee | 4 tbsp / 60 gm / 2 oz |
| Cumin (*jeera*) seeds | 1 tsp / 2 gm |
| Potatoes, peeled, diced | 4 cups / 600 gm / 22 oz |
| Green peas (*hara mater*) | 1½ cups / 150 gm / 5 oz |
| Turmeric (*haldi*) powder | ½ tsp / 1½ gm |
| Salt to taste | |
| Red chilli powder to taste | |
| Ginger (*adrak*) paste | 1 tbsp / 18 gm |
| Pomegranate seeds (*anar dana*), ground | 4 tsp / 12 gm |
| Vegetable oil for deep-frying | |

## Method

1. **For the pastry,** mix the refined flour, salt and oil together. Add enough water and knead into a semi-hard dough. Keep aside.
2. **For the filling,** heat the ghee in a wok (*kadhai*); sauté the cumin seeds for a minute. Add the vegetables, turmeric powder, salt, red chilli powder and ginger paste. Cook till the vegetables are done.
3. Add the pomegranate seeds and cook covered for 3-4 minutes. Remove from heat and keep aside to cool.
4. Divide the dough equally into 10 portions. Roll out each portion into 16 cm discs and then cut across the middle. Make a cone with each half in your palm. Place 1 tbsp of the filling in each cone. Pinch the edges to seal properly. Repeat till all the patties are done.
5. Heat the oil in a wok (*kadhai*); carefully lower the patties, a few at a time, and deep-fry in moderate heat. When the patties are cooked and golden brown, remove with a slotted spoon and drain the excess oil on absorbent kitchen towels.
6. Serve hot with coriander chutney (see p. 79) or tamarind chutney (see p. 167).

# SHAKARKANDI KI CHAAT  tangy sweet potatoes

serves: 4-6

## Ingredients

| | |
|---|---|
| Sweet potatoes (*shakarkandi*), boiled, cubed | 500 gm / 1.1 lb |
| Salt | 2 tsp / 8 gm |
| Tomatoes, chopped | 100 gm / 3½ oz |
| Lemon (*nimbu*) juice | 3 tbsp / 45 ml / 1½ fl oz |
| Green chillies, chopped | 4 |
| Green coriander (*hara dhaniya*), chopped | ½ cup / 25 gm |
| Mint (*pudina*) leaves, chopped | a few |
| Mango powder (*amchur*) | 2 tsp / 6 gm |

## Method

1. Mix salt, tomatoes, lemon juice, green chillies, green coriander, and mint leaves in a bowl. Add sweet potatoes and mix well.
2. Sprinkle mango powder over the mixture and serve.


# BESAN LADOO  sweet gram flour balls

makes: 10-12

## Ingredients

| | |
|---|---|
| Gram flour (*besan*) | 2½ cups / 250 gm / 9 oz |
| Ghee | 1 cup / 250 gm / 9 oz |
| Sugar, powdered | 1½ cups / 250 gm / 9 oz |

## Method

1. Heat the ghee in a wok (*kadhai*); add the gram flour and sauté till it turns brown.
2. Remove from heat and keep aside to cool.
3. When cool enough to handle, mix in the ghee and sugar and divide the mixture into 10-12 portions. Shape the portions into smooth balls.
4. Store in airtight containers. They remain fresh for several days.

**Right:** A sweet potato stand in one of south Delhi's posh shopping areas.

**Far Right:** Bottles of lime soda on display at a roadside stall in Rishikesh.

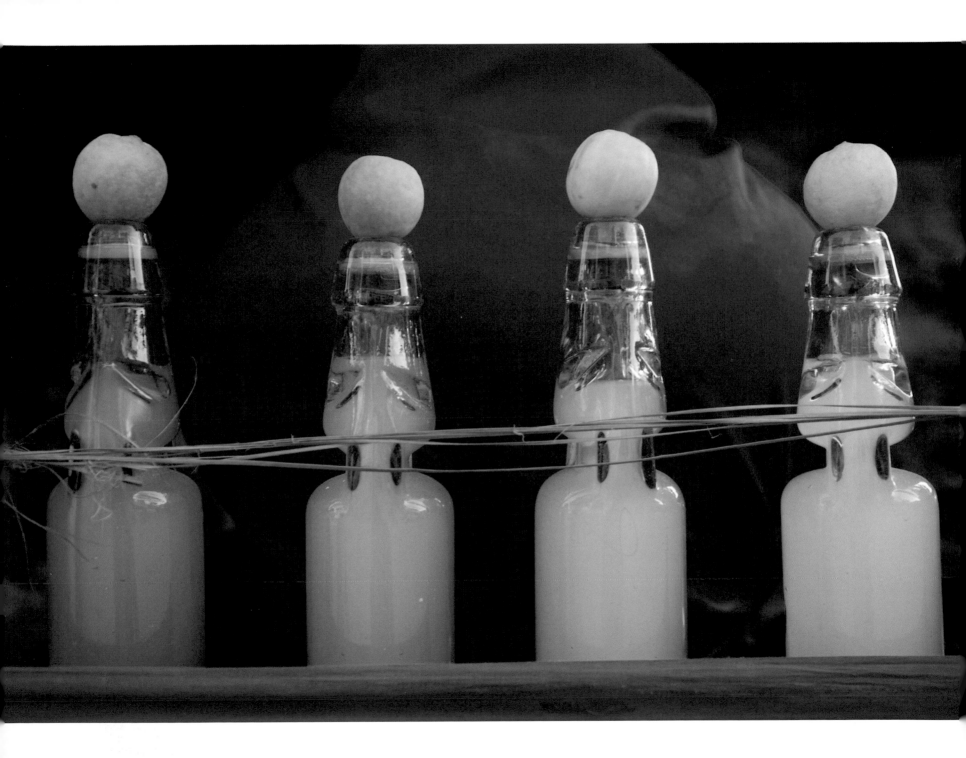

# BREAD PAKORA bread fritters

## Ingredients

| | |
|---|---|
| Bread slices | 4-5 |
| Gram flour (*besan*) | 1 cup / 100 gm / 3½ oz |
| Turmeric (*haldi*) powder | ¼ tsp |
| Salt to taste | |
| Carom seeds (*ajwain*) | ½ tsp |
| Red chilli powder to taste | |
| *Garam* masala | ¼ tsp |
| Water for batter | |
| Vegetable oil for frying | |

## Method

1. Cut the bread slices into desired shapes (like triangle, rectangle, etc.)
2. In a bowl, mix gram flour, turmeric powder, salt, carom seeds, red chilli powder, and *garam* masala.
3. Add a little water to make a smooth batter of coating consistency.
4. Heat the oil in a wok (*kadhai*); dip the bread slices in the batter and fry till crisp and golden brown on medium heat. Remove and drain the excess oil on absorbent kitchen towels.
5. Serve hot with green chutney (see p. 79) and tomato sauce.

Bread *pakora* garnished with chopped coriander and tamarind chutney.

A roadside *chai* stall in Kolkata.

Sweets, snacks and *chai* in *kulhar* (clay pots) in Kolkata.

# ALOO KI SUBZI  light potato curry

## Ingredients

| | |
|---|---|
| Potatoes, boiled, peeled, diced | 500 gm / 1.1 lb |
| Vegetable oil | 1 tbsp / 10 ml |
| Cumin (*jeera*) seeds | 1 tsp / 2 gm |
| Turmeric (*haldi*) powder | 2 tsp / 6 gm |
| Red chilli powder | 2 tsp / 6 gm |
| Salt to taste | |
| Water, hot | 3 cups / 750 ml / 24 fl oz |

## Method

1. Heat the oil in a wok (*kadhai*); add the cumin seeds, potatoes, turmeric powder, red chilli powder, salt and hot water. Mix well and cook for 15 minutes on medium flame or till the gravy is semi-thick.
2. Serve hot with *poori* (see below).

# POORI  deep-fried puffed wholewheat bread

serves: 4-6

## Ingredients

| | |
|---|---|
| Wholewheat flour (*atta*) | 2 cups / 300 gm / 11 oz |
| Salt | ½ tsp / 2 gm |
| Ghee | 2 tbsp / 30 gm / 1 oz |
| Water to knead | |
| Ghee / Vegetable oil for deep-frying | |

## Method

1. Combine all the ingredients together in a bowl (except oil) and knead into a stiff dough. Divide the dough into little balls; smear a bit of oil on each and roll into small discs not bigger than 5 cm or 2″ in diameter. Avoid using dry flour when rolling.
2. Heat the ghee or oil in a wok (*kadhai*); gently lower each disc and deep-fry. Press the disc with a flat slotted spoon, so that it puffs up. Then turn over and cook the other side till light golden. Remove at once and drain the excess oil on absorbent kitchen towels.

Two people eating *chhole bhature* (spicy chick peas served with deep-fried leavened bread) at a roadside eatery in Raipur.

**Pages 96-99**
The *paan* is closely connected to the Banarasi way of life, symbolizing the Banarasi's addiction to the good things of life. The betel leaf is stuffed with *supari* (areca nut), *katha* (catechu), *chuna* (lime), *gulkand* (rose jam), *elaichi* (cardamom) and for those who want it, tobacco. Eating a *paan*, folding it with spices and condiments and sharing it with a friend, is a gesture of hospitality. Visiting the roadside *paan-wala* to chew at leisure is an age-old habit that has been cultivated all over India. But in Banaras, *paan* is a tradition with a deep social significance.

**Pages 100-101**
**Left:** A gas-operated coffee machine in New Delhi.

**Right top:** A shop sign outside a coffee shop in Old Delhi.

**Right below:** Sweet cream rolls on offer in New Delhi.

A *paan* and cigarette shop near the railway station in Raipur.

**Left:** Close-up of a *paan* shop, Varanasi.

A street hawker selling *phirni* (creamy rice pudding) out of a 'cold box' on a cart on the streets of Amritsar.

Colourful bottles of sorbet on a street-cart and schoolboys enjoying *faluda* in a typical street scene in Amritsar.

# MOTH CHHOLE tangy sprouted gram   serves: 5-6

## Ingredients

| | |
|---|---|
| Chick peas (*kabuli chana*) | 1 cup / 150 gm / 5 oz |
| *Moth ki dal* | 1 cup / 200 gm / 7 oz |
| Tamarind chutney (*sonth*, see p. 167) | ½ cup / 100 gm / 3½ oz |
| Yoghurt (*dahi*) | ½ cup / 125 gm / 4 oz |
| Mint chutney (see p. 79) | ½ cup / 100 gm / 3½ oz |
| Onions, finely chopped | 2 |
| Green chillies, finely chopped | 2 |
| Green coriander (*hara dhaniya*), chopped for garnishing | |

## Method

1. Soak the pulses separately overnight. Pressure cook the chick peas till soft.
2. In a bowl, mix all the ingredients (except the green coriander) together.
3. Serve garnished with green coriander.

*Moth chhole* spiced with chutneys and vegetables served on dried leaves.

**Left:** A hawker carries a tray of *Ram ladoo* on his head and a portable stand on his shoulder in Lodi Gardens, New Delhi

**Far Left:** A serving of *Ram ladoo* (fried mixed gram fritters) and *mirchi pakora* (fried green chilli peppers) topped with radish and mint chutney in Lodi Gardens, New Delhi.

**Right:** Blessed by the gods: snacks on display at a roadside food stall in Kolkata.

**Far Right:** Lord Shiva painted on the wall as the backdrop of roadside food stall in Kolkata.

Crisp *samosas* (triangular vegetable patties) on the *tawa* (griddle), with the vendor frying the accompanying *aloo tikki* (potato patties) in hot oil, Mumbai.

**Right:** Golden-crusted *samosas* arranged to entice customers in a market in Old Delhi.

*Paans* wrapped in dried leaves, Old Delhi.

**Left:** *Kachoris* (stuffed deep-fried bread) wrapped in string against the backdrop of a picture of Lord Hanuman, Old Delhi.

Tastefully wrapped in *varq* (edible silver leaf) are these *mitha* (sweet) *paans* (betel leaf wrap). The *paan* has been used for generations for the digestive value of the green betel leaves. Betel nuts help strengthen the teeth and gums and *chuna* (calcium paste) is rich in calcium.

Most of the other contents which have slowly, over a period of centuries, made their way into the *paan* are for taste, with a few or no health benefits.

A hawker uses a portable machine to make sugarcane juice near Chandini Chowk in Old Delhi as people wait their turn for a drink.

The sweet green juice of sugarcane is a popular delicacy in India.

Irresistible cold *sharbat* (sweet drink) for sale at the Jama Masjid in Old Delhi.

**Left:** Glistening ruby-red pomegranates shown by a vendor on the streets of Hyderabad.

# CHOWMEIN vegetable noodles - Indian style

## Ingredients

| | |
|---|---|
| Noodles | 1 packet / 200 gm |
| Vegetable oil | 2 tbsp / 20 ml |
| Onion, finely sliced | 1 |
| Capsicum (*Shimla mirch*), sliced | 1 |
| Cabbage (*bandh gobi*), shredded | 1 |
| Carrot (*gajar*), sliced | 1 |
| French beans, chopped | ½ cup / 100 gm / 3½ oz |
| Soya sauce | 2 tbsp / 30 ml / 1 fl oz |
| Vinegar (*sirka*) | 2 tbsp / 30 ml / 1 fl oz |
| Chilli sauce to taste | |
| Salt to taste | |

## Method

1. Boil the noodles in enough water till soft but not overcooked. Wash the noodles 2-3 times in cold water; drain and keep aside. Add a few drops of oil to the noodles to avoid sticking.
2. Heat the oil in a wok (*kadhai*); add onion and stir-fry for 20-30 seconds. Add all the other vegetables and stir-fry for 2 minutes. Add salt and mix well.
3. Add the boiled noodles and mix well (taking care that the noodles don't break). Add soya sauce, vinegar, and chilli sauce; stir-fry for a minute.
4. Serve hot.

Office-goers enjoy lunch at a popular food stall in the financial district of Nariman Point in south Mumbai.

Seen here are *tuli*, the little twigs around which *kulfi* (home-made Indian ice-cream flavoured with ingredients, such as cardamom and pistachios) is frozen, and the knife used to slice the frozen chunks of ice-cream, on top of the cart of a *matka kulfi-wala* (an ice-cream-maker who uses a large *matka*, earthenware pot, to mix ingredients for his speciality), Ghaziabad.

A *matka kulfi-wala* looking for customers among the inhabitants of a government-housing complex in various stages of demolition, Ghaziabad.

# NIMBU PANI lemonade

serves: 4

## Ingredients

| | |
|---|---|
| Lemon (*nimbu*) juice | 1½ cups / 300 ml / 10 fl oz |
| Sugar | 2 cups / 440 gm / 15 oz |
| Water | 4 cups / 1 lt / 32 fl oz |
| Black salt (*kala namak*) | ½ tsp |
| Rind of lemon | 2 |
| Mint (*pudina*) leaves, chopped | 3 tbsp / 12 gm |

## Method

1. Dissolve the sugar in 1 cup of water and cook on low heat, stirring constantly to make syrup of one-string consistency. Remove and keep aside to cool.
2. Add lemon juice and 3 cups of water. Mix and add black salt and lemon rind just before serving.
3. Alternatively, one can also use club soda instead of water. Serve garnished with mint leaves.

Cold drink, coloured a garish yellow, for sale at the Jama Masjid, Old Delhi.

A hawker selling *kulfi* to tourists at the Gateway of India in Mumbai.

People savouring *kulfi* on Chowpatty Beach, Mumbai.

**Right:** Buttered delight: A popcorn cart's window in south Delhi.

**Far Right:** A veteran vendor tries to tempt a young customer to buy popcorn at Chowpatty Beach, Mumbai.

**Left Above:** People enjoy spiced, roasted corn-on-the-cob on Juhu beach in Mumbai.

**Left Below:** A man taking his *chai* (tea) to passers-by from a portable *chai* stall, Chowpatty Beach in Mumbai.

**Far Left:** Hawkers on Chowpatty Beach sell cotton sugar, coloured a vivid pink, called *budia ke bal* (old woman's hair), Mumbai.

# KULFI home made Indian ice cream

## Ingredients

| | |
|---|---|
| Full-cream milk | 4 cups / 1 lt / 32 fl oz |
| Sugar | 4 tbsp / 60 gm / 2 oz |
| Green cardamom (*choti elaichi*), powdered | 3 |
| Cream, thick, whipped | ½ cup / 120 ml / 4 fl oz |
| Pistachios (*pista*), peeled, slivered | 50 gm / 1¾ oz |
| Silver leaf (*varq*), optional | |

## Method

1. Boil the milk and sugar together, stirring frequently, on low heat until reduced to half. Remove and cool.
2. Stir in the green cardamom powder and cream. Sprinkle the pistachios and mix well. Pour into dry *kulfi* cones, leaving 5 cm of empty space on top. Turn the cover tightly and stand on its base. Similarly, fill the other cones and leave overnight, to freeze.
3. Before serving, roll the *kulfi* cone between the palms or dip for a minute in hot water. Open the cover and then slide into a small bowl.
4. Garnish with silver leaf and/or pistachios, if desired. Serve at once.

**Right:** Impatient to get hold of the two ice-cream cones his father holds tantalizingly above him, a young boy waits in anticipation.

**Left:** A vendor holding two leaf-plates with cold *kulfi* in the narrow lanes of Old Delhi.

**Right:** Spicy roasted corn-on-the-cob, known as *bhutta* in India, is best made with yellow corn with kernels that are not too soft. Each vendor has his own secret recipe of spices which he applies generously to the roasted corn.

**Far Right:** A *bhutta* (corn) vendor outside Gurudwara Damdama Sahib, New Delhi.

# BHUTTA SIKA HUA corn-on-the-cob serves: 6

## Ingredients

| | |
|---|---|
| Corns (*bhutta*), fresh, tender, peeled | 6 |
| Butter, optional | |
| Salt | 3 tsp / 12 gm |
| Red chilli powder | 2 tsp / 6 gm |
| Lemon (*nimbu*), halved | 1 |

## Method

1. Place the corn directly on the fire. Keep rotating it so that it cooks evenly. Remove when brown.
2. Smear with butter, salt and red chilli powder and rub the lemon over it.
3. Serve warm.

**Note:** The best result is obtained by cooking the corn on embers of charcoal fire or the barbecue.

Street side vendors frantically fan their mobile coal fires to gently roast *bhutta* (corn cobs) while people line up to buy this popular Indian snack.

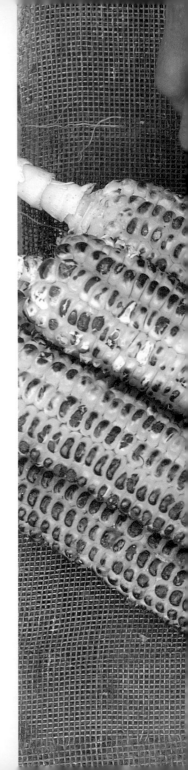

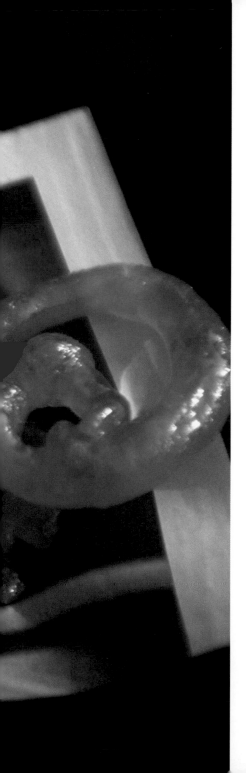

# JALEBI  sweet flour whirls

serves: 4-6

## Ingredients

| | |
|---|---|
| Refined flour (*maida*) | 6 tbsp / 60 gm / 2 oz |
| Gram flour (*besan*) | 2 tbsp / 20 gm |
| Yoghurt (*dahi*) | 2 tbsp / 30 gm / 1 oz |
| Vegetable oil | 1 tbsp / 10 ml |
| Water | ½ cup / 125 ml / 4 fl oz |
| Sugar | 1¼ cups / 280 gm / 10 oz |
| Vegetable oil for deep-frying | |

## Method

1. Mix the refined flour, gram flour, yoghurt, oil and water together and let it ferment overnight.
2. Make the syrup with the water and sugar till a one-string consistency is achieved. Keep aside.
3. Heat the oil in a flat pan. Beat the mixture thoroughly and pack it in a plastic bag. Cut a small hole in one corner and slowly press the bag over the hot oil. Try to make 6 cm whirls starting from the outer ring and ending at the centre. Fry till both sides are crisp. To turn over, use a steel or bamboo skewer. Remove gently with tongs and drain.
4. Soak them in sugar syrup for about 4 minutes and then remove. Serve hot.

Sweet, hot, crisp *jalebis*, dripping syrup, are a well-appreciated delicacy on the streets of Delhi. They are served in a paper plate or simply on a piece of paper.

**Left Above:** People jostling to buy *gulab jamuns* at a popular food stall in Old Delhi.

**Left Below:** A sweet vendor in Old Delhi selling *gajar ka halwa* (a sweet confection made of carrots and *khoya*, thickened whole milk) and *gulab jamuns* (a popular Indian sweet dish of fried milk balls in a syrup flavoured with cardamom seeds and rose water or saffron. It may have originated from eastern India, Orissa or Bengal). The art of making *halwa* with nuts was introduced in India during the Mughal period by the traders from the Middle East and Asia. Indian cooks are credited with making *halwa* by using vegetables such as carrots, pumpkin, zucchini, snake squash, winter melon, potatoes, and yams. This glazed carrot *halwa*, a speciality of the Sikhs of Punjab, is very popular in India.

**Far Left:** Syrupy delight: Glistening *gulab jamuns* simmering gently in a cauldron.

# GULAB JAMUN  fried cottage cheese dumplings

makes: 25

## Ingredients

**For the dumplings:**

| | |
|---|---|
| Full-cream milk powder | 2 cups / 300 gm / 11 oz |
| Self-raising flour (*maida*) | 1 cup / 140 gm / 4½ oz |
| Semolina (*suji*), fine | ½ cup / 50 gm / 1¾ oz |
| Thickened cream to knead | |
| Vegetable oil for deep-frying | |

**For sugar syrup:**

| | |
|---|---|
| Sugar | 2¼ cups / 500 gm / 1.1 lb |
| Water | 3 cups / 750 ml / 24 fl oz |
| Rose water (*gulab jal*) | 3 tsp / 15 ml |

## Method

1. **For the dumplings,** mix all the ingredients and knead with a light touch to form a soft dough. Divide the mixture into 25 portions and shape each into balls.
2. **For sugar syrup,** boil the water and sugar till the sugar dissolves completely and the syrup is of one-string consistency when tested between the thumb and index finger. When cool, stir in rose water.
3. Heat the oil in a wok (*kadhai*); carefully lower a few balls, at a time, gently shaking the oil constantly so that they become uniformly brown. Remove and immerse them in sugar syrup. Repeat until all the balls are fried. Soak the dumplings for an hour in the syrup.
4. Serve warm (30 seconds on medium high in the microwave).

---

# PHIRNI  creamy rice pudding

serves: 4-6

## Ingredients

| | |
|---|---|
| Rice, Basmati, soaked for an hour | 3 tbsp |
| Full-cream milk | 4 cups / 1 lt / 32 fl oz |
| Sugar | 1 cup / 220 gm / 8 oz |
| Rose water (*gulab jal*) | 1 tbsp / 15 ml |
| Almonds (*badam*), blanched, finely chopped | 15 |
| Pistachios (*pista*), finely chopped | 10 |
| Saffron (*kesar*), soaked in 1 tbsp water | 10 strands |
| Green cardamom (choti elaichi), crushed | 4-5 |
| Silver leaves (*varq*) | 4-5 |

## Method

1. Grind the rice with ½ cup water.
2. Heat the milk in a pan; add the rice paste and keep stirring till it thickens enough to coat the back of a spoon. Add the sugar and cook till the mixture thickens again to coat the back of the spoon.
3. Remove from heat and transfer the thickened milk into individual earthen containers or glass bowls.
4. Sprinkle rose water and dry fruits.
5. Grind the saffron in a mortar and pestle. Sprinkle this over the dry fruits along with green cardamom powder.
6. Serve decorated with silver leaves

# PARATHA  unleavened fried bread

makes: 5

## Ingredients

| | |
|---|---|
| Wholewheat flour (*atta*) | 3⅓ cups / 500 gm / 1.1 lb |
| Salt to taste | |
| Ghee | 1 cup / 250 gm / 9 oz |
| Water | 1 cup / 250 ml / 8 fl oz |

## Method

1. Sift the wholewheat flour and salt in a bowl, incorporate 2 tbsp ghee, add the water gradually, and knead to a smooth dough.
2. Divide the dough into 5 equal portions and shape into balls. Dust each with flour, cover with a damp cloth and keep aside for 10 minutes.
3. Flatten each ball and roll out. Brush with ghee and fold over. Brush the folded surface with ghee and fold over again to form a triangle. Roll out the triangle with a rolling pin.
4. Heat a griddle (*tawa*) and brush the surface with ghee. Place the *paratha* on the griddle and fry for a few minutes. Coat with a little ghee, turn over and fry the other side as well. Both sides of the *paratha* should be crisp and delicately browned.
5. Remove and serve immediately.

# NAMKEEN LASSI  salted yoghurt drink

serves: 4

## Ingredients

| | |
|---|---|
| Yoghurt (*dahi*) | 2 cups / 500 gm / 1.1 lb |
| Cumin (*jeera*) seeds, roasted, powdered | 1 tsp / 2 gm |
| Water | 4 cups / 1 lt / 32 fl oz |
| Salt | ¼ tsp |
| Black salt (*kala namak*) | ¼ tsp |
| Ice cubes, crushed | |
| *Chaat* masala, optional | ½ tsp |

## Method

Blend the first five ingredients till frothy. Add the crushed ice and *chaat* masala (optional), serve immediately.

*Phirni* (a creamy rice pudding) set in earthenware plates and decorated with silver leaf and pistachios, Amritsar.

**Left:** A man selling *phirni* in small earthenware pots on the streets of Old Delhi.

Eager customers unable to wait even a second for a cup of steaming, sweet tea. The number of glasses that a *chai-wala* (tea vendor) has, and the number of litres of milk that he finishes, indicates the quality of the *chai* he makes.

Ustad Tea Stall is a popular tea stall in Old Delhi near the Jama Masjid where the *chai-wala* makes tea with *malai* (cream). I call it 'Chai Latté' and this is the only place in India to get it.

**Left:** On a winter night in Old Delhi, hot milk is mixed to be used for masala *chai* at a tea stall.

**Far Left:** The *chai-wala* (tea vendor) is a well-entrenched street entrepreneur in Delhi. Indian masala tea is a unique concoction of milk and ginger, cardamom and cloves.

A glimpse of culinary heaven through the window of an eatery in Parathe Wali Gali, a lane renowned for its immense variety of *parathas* (unleavened fried bread stuffed with an infinite range of combinations of vegetables) in Old Delhi.

An evening crowd gathers near a favourite eating joint, presided over by an image of Lord Shiva, in Old Delhi.

On the last day of Ramadan, a temporary food stall is set up near the gate of the Jama Masjid, in Old Delhi, to sell *halwa paratha*, a famous combination of sweet fried bread and confectionery, to people coming out of the mosque after the break of the fast.

Giant *paratha* (unleavened fried bread), probably the biggest thing you will ever see coming out a frying pan. It is then cut into smaller pieces and served with the sweet *halwa*.

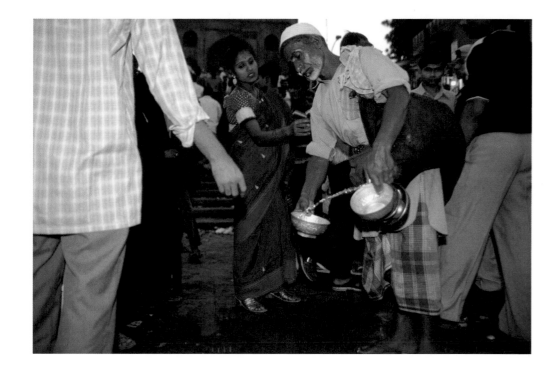

A *bisthi* (a water-vendor), selling water out of a goatskin to people outside the Jama Masjid, Old Delhi.

**Left:** Reason to smile: The sun sets behind the Jama Masjid in Old Delhi as a vendor prepares yet another serving of *biryani* (rice cooked with meat and fragrant spices) which he skillfully weighs into an exact measure, using a simple hand scale.

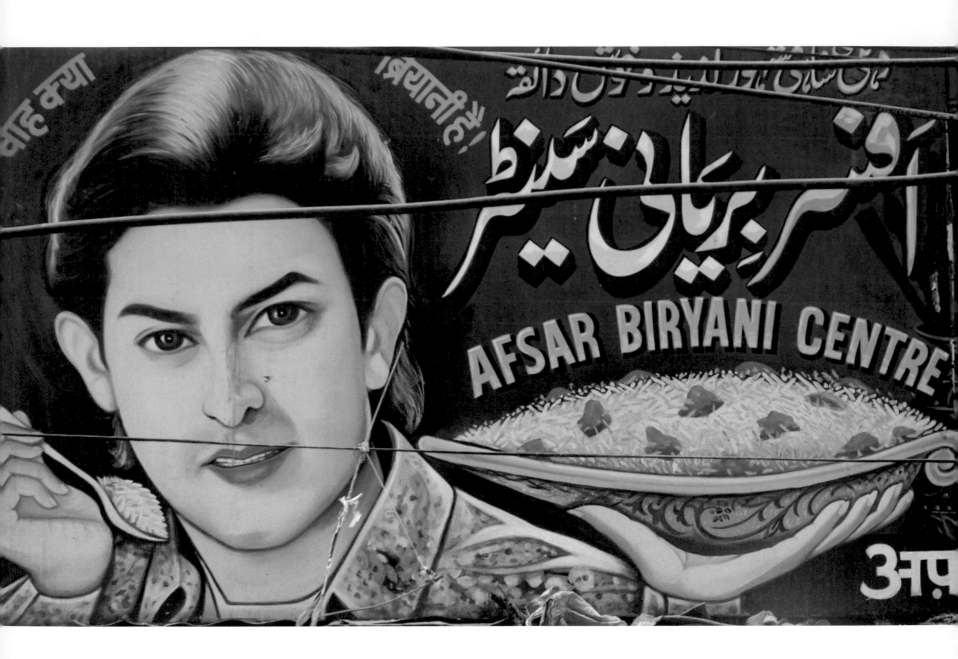

# SUBZ BIRYANI  seasoned vegetable rice

## Ingredients

| | |
|---|---:|
| Rice, Basmati | 1 cup / 200 gm / 7 oz |
| Carrot (*gajar*), diced, parboiled | 30 gm / 1 oz |
| Cauliflower (*phool gobi*), small pieces | 30 gm / 1 oz |
| Green peas (*hara mater*), parboiled | 30 gm / 1 oz |
| Mushrooms (*guchhi*), quartered | 30 gm / 1 oz |
| Vegetable oil | 6 tbsp / 60 ml / 2 fl oz |
| Cloves (*laung*) | 4 |
| Cinnamon (*dalchini*), ½'' stick | 1 |
| Bay leaf (*tej patta*) | 1 |
| Green cardamom (*choti elaichi*) | 3 |
| Black cumin seeds (*shah jeera*) | 1 tsp / 2½ gm |
| Onions, chopped | 30 gm / 1 oz |
| Ginger (*adrak*) paste | 2 tsp / 12 gm |
| Red chilli powder | 1 tsp / 3 gm |
| White pepper (*safed mirch*) powder | ½ tsp / 1½ gm |
| Salt to taste | |
| Water | 2 cups / 500 ml / 16 fl oz |

**For the garnishing:**

| | |
|---|---:|
| Green chillies, slit | 1 tsp |
| Onion, sliced, fried | 2 tsp / 12 gm |
| Mace (*javitri*) powder | ½ tsp / 1½ gm |
| Lemon (*nimbu*) juice | 1 tbsp / 15 ml |
| Ginger, julienned | ½ tsp / 3 gm |
| Cashew nuts (*kaju*), fried golden | 10 |
| Green coriander (*hara dhaniya*), chopped | 1 tbsp / 4 gm |
| Cream | 2 tbsp / 30 ml / 1 fl oz |

## Method

1. Wash and soak the rice for 30 minutes.
2. Heat the oil in a heavy-bottomed pan, sauté the cloves, cinnamon stick, bay leaf, green cardamom, and black cumin seeds till they begin to crackle.
3. Add onions and sauté till transparent. Stir in ginger paste, red chilli powder, all the vegetables, white pepper powder, and salt. Cook for 3-4 minutes.
4. Stir in the drained rice and water. Bring to the boil, lower heat and cook, covered, till rice is almost done.
5. Remove the lid, sprinkle slit green chillies, fried onions, mace powder, lemon juice, ginger, cashew nuts, green coriander, and cream.
6. Seal the lid with dough and cook on very low heat for 10-15 minutes.
7. Serve hot with yoghurt.

Colourful sign over a shop selling *biryani* in Old Delhi.

**Left:** A *chana jor garam* (a mouth-watering Indian traditional snack made out of black gram) vendor near Victoria Memorial, Kolkata.

**Far Left:** *Chana jor garam* rolled up in a paper cone made of an old newspaper in Rishikesh.

A tray of *longlata*, a kind of sweet, on display in one of Mumbai's neighbourhoods. A smoke stick stands vigilantly to drive away flies.

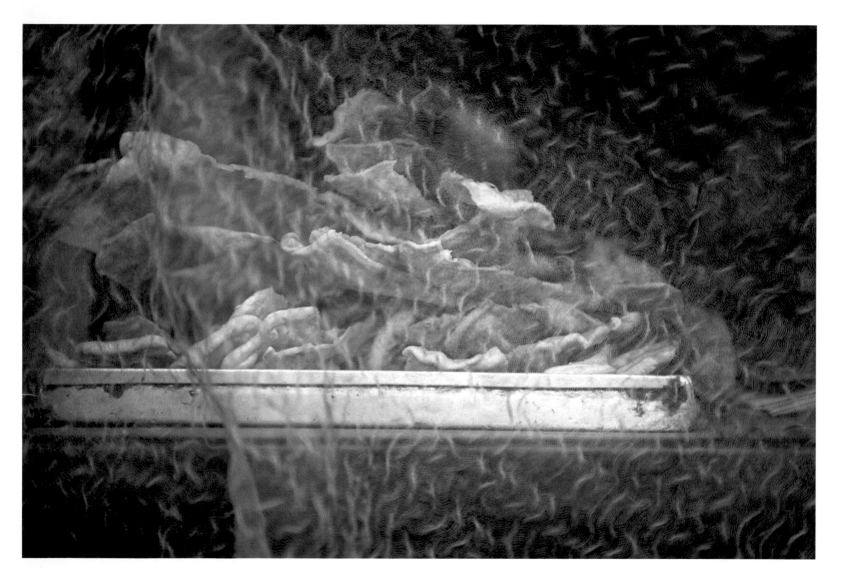

*Papri* (flour crispies) behind a blue net to protect the snack from the flies, Mumbai.

**Right:** An old man walks by a *moongphalli* (groundnuts) vendor selling his wares at a ghat in Varanasi.

**Far Right:** On the last day of Ramadan, vendors at a meat shop stack up fried chicken in anticipation of hungry customers after the break of the fast outside Jama Masjid in Old Delhi.

Paniuri or *pani puri*, is a snack synonymous with the beaches of Mumbai. It is also very popular in all other parts of India and known by many names such as *golgappa* in north India, *foochka* (*puchka*) in West Bengal or *gupchup* in some central parts of India like Hyderabad or Chhattisgarh. Made of semolina (*suji*) or whole-wheat flour (*atta*), the puffed *puri* is stuffed with potato and chick-peas and then dipped in tamarind sauce and cold cumin water (*jal jeera*). In other parts of India it comes with *kali mirch pani* (black pepper water), *pudina pani* (mint water), *nimbu pani* (lemonade), *hing pani* (asafoetida) or *imli* and *dahi* (tamarind sauce and yoghurt).

**Left:** *Golgappa* dipped in *jal jeera* (cumin water). To eat it without the mess of the water spilling out, the whole *puri* has to be popped into the mouth in one bite.

**Far Left:** On a hot summer day, people enjoy chilled *golgappa* from a street vendor in the by-lanes of Old Delhi.

# GOLGAPPA  stuffed deep-fried puffs filled with tamarind water                  serves: 4-6

## Ingredients

**For the *golgappa*:**

| | |
|---|---|
| Refined flour (*maida*) | 2 cups / 280 gm / 10 oz |
| Semolina (*suji*) | 1 cup / 100 gm / 3½ oz |
| Cold water to knead | |

**Filling for the *golgappa*:**

| | |
|---|---|
| Sprouted brown gram, boiled | 2 tbsp |
| Potatoes, boiled, peeled, diced | 100 gm / 3½ oz |

**For the tamarind water:**

| | |
|---|---|
| Cold water | 6 cups / 1½ lt |
| Cumin (*jeera*) powder | 3 tsp / 9 gm |
| Tamarind (*imli*), soaked for 30 minutes in 1 cup water, strained | 1 tbsp / 6 gm |
| Black salt (*kala namak*) | 1½ tsp / 6 gm |
| Black pepper (*kali mirch*) powder | 2 tsp / 6 gm |
| Ginger (*adrak*) paste | 2 tsp / 12 gm |
| Mint (*pudina*) leaves, chopped | 1 cup / 35 gm / 1¼ oz |

**To serve with *papri*:**

| | |
|---|---|
| Chick peas (*kabuli chana*), cooked | 1 tbsp |
| Potatoes, medium-sized, boiled, peeled, diced | 2 |
| Yoghurt (*dahi*), whipped | ½ cup / 125 gm / 4 oz |
| *Chaat* masala | 3 tsp / 9 gm |
| Red chilli powder | ½ tsp / 1½ gm |
| Tamarind sauce | 3 tbsp / 45 gm / 1½ oz |

## Method

1. **For the *golgappa* and *papri*,** mix the flour and semolina with water and knead to a stiff dough. Divide the dough equally and make 3 cm balls. Roll each ball out into thick rounds. Cover with a damp cloth and keep aside.
2. Deep-fry the rounds till crisp and puffed up. Remove with a slotted spoon and keep aside. **Papri** is made in the same way except that the rolled out rounds are pricked with a fork before frying, so that they remain crisp and flat.
3. **For the tamarind water,** mix all the ingredients with the water and stir well. Keep this water in a ceramic jug.
4. **To serve *golgappas*,** make a small hole in the centre of the puffed up ball, put in a couple of sprouted brown gram, a little potato and fill with the tamarind water. It should be eaten whole and immediately.
5. Serve the ***papris*** with the chick pea, potatoes, yoghurt, sprinkled with *chaat* masala, red chilli powder and tamarind sauce.

# JAL JEERA  tangy cumin water

## Ingredients

| | |
|---|---|
| Ice water | 3 cups / 750 ml / 24 fl oz |
| Lemon (*nimbu*) juice | 2 tbsp / 30 ml / 1 fl oz |
| Cumin (*jeera*) powder | 1 tbsp / 9 gm |
| Mint (*pudina*) paste | 1 tsp / 5 gm |
| Black salt (*kala namak*) | ½ tsp |
| Sugar | ¼ tsp |
| Mint leaves for garnishing | |

## Method

1. Mix everything together and serve chilled with ice. Garnish with fresh mint.

It is recommended to keep the mixture in the refrigerator for one day to let all the flavours blend in.

# SONTH  tamarind chutney

makes: 10-12

## Ingredients

| | |
|---|---|
| Tamarind (*imli*) or | 8 tbsp / 50 gm |
|   Tamarind concentrate | 5 tbsp / 30 gm |
| Sugar or | 1-1½ tbsp / 15-22 gm |
|   Jaggery, chopped | 1-1½ tbsp / 20-30 gm |
| Cumin (*jeera*) seeds, roasted, powdered | 10 tsp / 20 gm |
| Red chilli powder | 1 tsp / 3 gm |
| Black salt (*kala namak*), optional | ½ tsp |

## Method

1. Soak the tamarind in 2 cups of hot water for 30 minutes. Press and strain the pulp out. If using tamarind concentrate, mix 2 cups of hot water in the concentrate to get a smooth sauce. Boil either the tamarind juice or the tamarind sauce with the sugar or jaggery until thick.
2. When thick, mix in the cumin powder, red chilli powder and black salt. Serve cold.

**Left:** A man carries a tray of *golgappa* on his head and a chair on his arm on way to the spot where he will put up his stand for the evening, Kolkata.

**Far Left:** A *golgappa* vendor and his portable stall on the way to catering for eager customers, Mumbai.

# BHEL PURI  tangy puffed rice mixture

## Ingredients

| | |
|---|---|
| Puffed rice (*murmura*) | ½ cup / 50 gm / 1¾ oz |
| Gram flour (*besan*) or chick pea vermicelli | ½ cup / 50 gm / 1¾ oz |
| **For the flat pastries:** | |
| Wholewheat flour (*atta*) | ½ cup / 75 gm / 2½ oz |
| Semolina (*suji*) | ½ cup / 100 gm / 3½ oz |
| Onion seeds (*kalonji*), powdered | 1 tsp / 3 gm |
| Salt to taste | |
| Vegetable oil | 1 tsp / 5 ml |
| **For the mint chutney:** | |
| Mint (*pudina*) leaves, discard stems | 250 gm / 9 oz |
| Onions, medium-sized, peeled, chopped | 2 |
| Green chillies, chopped | 3 |
| Lemon (*nimbu*) juice | 1 tbsp / 15 ml |
| Salt to taste | |
| Sugar, optional | 2 tsp / 6 gm |
| Water, cold | 1 cup / 250 ml / 8 fl oz |
| | |
| Potatoes, medium-sized, boiled, peeled, diced | 2 |
| Onion, medium-sized, chopped | 1 |
| Tamarind chutney (see p. 167) | |

## Method

1. Mix the puffed rice, gram flour or chick pea vermicelli together. Keep aside.
2. **For the flat pastries** (*papri*), mix the wholewheat flour, semolina, onion seed powder and salt. Knead with water to form a medium-soft dough. Divide the dough equally into marble-sized balls. Roll each out thinly without coating with flour. Then prick all over with a fork.
3. Heat the oil in a wok (*kadhai*); deep-fry the discs, a few at a time. When golden and crisp on both sides remove with a slotted spoon. Drain the excess oil on absorbent kitchen towels. Repeat until all are done.
4. **For the mint chutney**, grind or blend all the ingredients together with water to make a thick, smooth paste. Keep aside.
5. Add the flat pastries, potatoes and onions to the puffed rice mixture.
6. Now, add the mint chutney and tamarind chutney, mix well and serve immediately.

Synonymous with Mumbai is *bhel puri*, a must-have culinary delight on the Chowpatty Beach, and *batata puri* (fried semolina bread drenched with yoghurt and spices); both are popular snacks throughout India.

A hawker selling *masala muri* and *bhel puri* as evening falls on the Maidan near Victoria Memorial, Kolkata.

A young boy selling *moongphalli* (groundnuts) at night in the *mela* grounds on the dry riverbed of the river Ganga during the Maha Kumbh Mela in Allahabad.

**Right:** *Bhel puri* (tangy puffed rice mixture) stall in front of Victoria Memorial, Kolkata.

Left: A shop in Delhi selling cold *lassi*.

Far Left: *Thandai* is another Varanasi speciality. It is a cooling drink made of purified water, sugar, seeds of watermelon and musk melon, almonds, lotus stem seeds, cashew nut, cardamom, aniseed, rose-flower, white pepper, saffron and *bhang*. *Bhang* is an intoxicant made from a leaf that grows wild in Uttar Pradesh and Bihar, like opium and marijuana, but which farmers need a government license to cultivate and sell. A spoon of *bhang* in the *thandai* makes a world of a difference. *Bhang* is mixed with milk, ice and cream, and added to the *thandai* to produce a kick!

A man frying *aloo tikki* (potato patties), at night in Old Delhi.

**Right:** *Aloo tikkis* sizzling to a crisp finish.

# ALOO TIKKI  fried potato patties

## Ingredients

| | |
|---|---|
| Potatoes, large, washed, boiled, peeled, mashed | 1 kg / 2.2 lb |
| Vegetable oil | 3 tbsp / 30 ml / 1 fl oz |
| Green gram (*moong dal*), soaked for | |
|   30 minutes | 1¼ cups / 250 gm / 9 oz |
| Turmeric (*haldi*) powder | 2 tsp / 6 gm |
| Red chilli powder | 1 tsp / 3 gm |
| Cumin (*jeera*) seeds, lightly roasted, powdered | 3 tsp / 6 gm |
| Salt to taste | |
| Water | 1 cup / 250 ml / 8 fl oz |
| Mango powder (*amchur*) | 1 tsp / 3 gm |
| Vegetable oil / Ghee for shallow-frying | |

## Method

1. Heat the oil in a pan; add the green gram, turmeric powder, red chilli powder, cumin powder, salt and water. Cook covered on medium heat until almost done.
2. Add the mango powder and cook for a few more minutes, ensuring that the green gram grains remain intact. A little more water may be added, if required. Keep aside.
3. To the mashed potatoes, add salt to taste. Divide this equally into lemon-sized portions. Grease your palms and roll each portion between your palms to make a ball, then flatten into a smooth, round patty about ½" thick. Put 2 tsp of the green gram filling in the centre. Fold the edges together and seal the filling inside. Flatten again with the fingers to a 3 cm thickness. Keep aside and shape all the pieces this way.
4. Heat a few drops of oil / ghee on a griddle (*tawa*) or a non-stick frying pan; lay the patties flat on it. Cook on medium heat, adding a few drops of oil around the edges. Turn over when deep red and crisp. Repeat on the other side. Remove and drain the excess oil on absorbent kitchen towels.
5. Serve hot with mint chutney (see p. 79) or tamarind chutney (see p. 167).

# AAMLETTE  spicy omelette

## Ingredients

| | |
|---|---|
| Eggs | 6 |
| Salt to taste | |
| Black pepper (*kali mirch*) powder to taste | |
| Red chilli powder to taste | |
| Vegetable oil | 3-4 tbsp / 30-40 ml / 1-1¼ fl oz |
| Green chillies, chopped | 1 tbsp |
| Onions, chopped | 1 cup / 240 gm / 9 oz |

## Method

1. Break the eggs in a bowl and beat till frothy. Mix in the salt, black pepper powder and red chilli powder.
2. Heat 1 tbsp oil in a flat frying pan; pour half the egg mixture, reduce heat and sprinkle half the green chillies and onion. As the mixture dries, slowly turn it over. Cook for another minute. Remove, cut into 3 pieces and serve while still hot. Repeat till all the egg mixture is used up.
3. Serve with chilli or tomato sauce.

---

# MASALA CHAI  flavoured tea

## Ingredients

| | |
|---|---|
| Water | 6 cups / 1½ lt |
| Tea leaves or tea dust | 4 tsp |
| Ginger (*adrak*), roughly chopped | 1 tsp / 7½ gm |
| Green cardamom (*choti elaichi*), powdered | 2 |
| Milk | ½ cup / 125 ml / 4 fl oz |
| Sugar to taste, optional | |

## Method

1. Boil the water, tea leaves, ginger and green cardamom powder together for 3 minutes. Add the milk and sugar (optional) and boil for another 2 minutes.
2. Strain through a fine wire mesh strainer and serve at once.

Close to midnight, on a street otherwise busy with heavy traffic, people grab a quick night bite from a passing *anda-wala* selling eggs and egg sandwiches, New Delhi.

**Left:** An egg stall in Old Delhi. The *bun-anda* (egg sandwich) vendor selling eggs is one of India's best-known entrepreneurs on whom office goers and night birds depend.

**Left:** Indian masala tea is prepared with milk, ginger, cardamom and cloves and has a distinctive taste. One can have a glass of *chai* at any time of day and night in Delhi.

**Far Left:** A roadside tea stall near Talala, Gujarat.

There is nothing fancy about drinking tea in India. Tea drinking, for the average India, means a few whiffs, a couple of slurps, and a final gulp of the sticky-sweet, over-boiled milky drink at a road-side *chai-wala*.

In Gujarat it is sipped from plates and not cups, to cool the hot liquid quickly.

After other shops close, a sweet vendor sells *gulab jamuns and barfi* (sweet fudge) and other delicacies from a make-shift stall on the sidewalk in the alleys behind the Jama Masjid in Old Delhi.

A vendor selling spicy *kachoris* in the alleys of Old Delhi. The *kachori* has many avatars, but it is basically a flavoured crispy wheat puff, stuffed with potato, peas and lentils. It is sold in leaf plates accompanied by a dry chick pea preparation called *ghoogny* (a spicy dry pea curry).

# PANEER TIKKA grilled cottage cheese cubes

## Ingredients

| | |
|---|---|
| Cottage cheese (*paneer*) | 1 kg / 2.2 lb |
| Black cumin seeds (*shah jeera*) | 1 tsp / 2½ gm |
| White pepper (*safed mirch*) powder | 1 tsp / 3 gm |
| *Garam* masala | 2 tsp / 6 gm |
| Lemon (*nimbu*) juice | 5 tsp / 25 ml |
| Salt to taste | |
| Cottage cheese, grated | 50 gm / 1¾ oz |
| Cream | ½ cup / 120 ml / 4 fl oz |
| Yoghurt (*dahi*), hung | ½ cup / 125 gm / 4 oz |
| Gram flour (*besan*) / Cornflour | 2 tbsp / 20 gm |
| Dry fenugreek leaves (*kasoori methi*) | 4 tsp / 2 gm |
| *Chaat* masala, optional | 2 tsp / 6 gm |
| Ginger-garlic (*adrak-lasan*) paste | 2 tbsp / 36 gm / 1¼ oz |
| Red chilli powder | 2 tsp / 6 gm |
| Butter for basting | |

## Method

1. Wash and cut the cottage cheese into 4 cm or 1½'' cubes.
2. Mix black cumin seeds, white pepper powder, *garam* masala, 4 tsp lemon juice, salt, and grated cottage cheese together. Marinate the cottage cheese cubes in this mixture; refrigerate for an hour.
3. Whisk the remaining ingredients (except butter) to a fine batter. Add the cottage cheese cubes, mix well and marinate for at least an hour.
4. Pre-heat the oven to 150°C / 300°F. Thread the cubes 2 cm or 1" apart on a skewer. Roast in an oven / charcoal grill for 5-6 minutes basting with butter.
5. Serve hot sprinkled with *chaat* masala and remaining lemon juice and accompanied with mint chutney (see p. 79).

A delicious grilled dish made of *paneer*. *Paneer* is firm Indian cheese which soaks up the flavour of any marinade and keeps its shape when cooked.

A *rickshaw-wala* (a rickshaw driver) stops for ice-cream on the side of the road at night in New Delhi. Ice-cream vendors will stay up all night during summer, waiting for a car to pull over and buy an occasional ice-cream cone.

An ice-cream vendor near the India Gate, New Delhi. Hundreds of such carts set up here attract crowds on summer nights.

Night at Haridwar railway station. A hawker pushes his mobile shop along the tracks, offering fresh fried *puri* (puffed wheat bread) to the passengers on the train.

Sustenance for travellers at night: Wakeful vendors ready to offer *chai* (tea) at night at Haridwar railway station.

# acknowledgements

I would like to thank the following persons for their help and encouragement in the making of this book:

Hanoch Bar Shalom, for a long distance call that started the whole thing;

Sébastien Bizeul who encouraged me to pick up my camera again after a long break;

Rishab Ratnu, who was the first to tell me that the images make him hungry, for his wonderful ideas and friendship;

Mr. Carlo Donatti from Nestlé India, and Dr. Alka Pande from the India Habitat Centre, for their help with my first exhibition in India that gave a considerable push to the project;

Sourabh Ratnu, for some Mumbai magic;

my good friend George Kurian, for spending hours with me over the images and their stories;

Inga Butefisch from Down Under who called me a 'Dill' for not writing, and helped with the text;

my friend, my brother, Felix Tamus who is always there for me;

to my dear wife Shefi, for her love, her support and her patience;

and my daughter Liah, for being the light of my life.

This book is dedicated to my late mother, Hava Lev (Bergerson) who I'm sure, as a good 'Yidishe Mame' would be very proud.

BABA NAM KEVALAM